Bret Ludwick and Casey Trout are long time friends with similar creativity. They both hail from Northern Colorado.

These Are My Faces

by

Bret J. Ludwick

AUSTIN MACAULEY PUBLISHERS™

LONDON * CAMBRIDGE * NEW YORK * SHARJAH

Copyright © Bret J. Ludwick (2018)

Ordering Information:

Quantity sales: special discounts are available on quantity purchases by corporations, associations, and others. For details, contact the publisher at the address below.

Ludwick, Bret J.
These Are My Faces

ISBN 9781641829922 (Paperback)
ISBN 9781641829939 (Hardback)
ISBN 9781641829946 (E-Book)

The main category of the book — Family & relationships

www.austinmacauley.com/us

First Published (2018)
Austin Macauley Publishers LLC
40 Wall Street, 28th Floor
New York, NY 10005
USA

mail-usa@austinmacauley.com
+1 (646) 5125767

To London and Brooks Ludwick, and all the people that love art.

this is my love face

this is my mad face

this is my sad face

this
is
my
excited
face

this is my
swimming
face

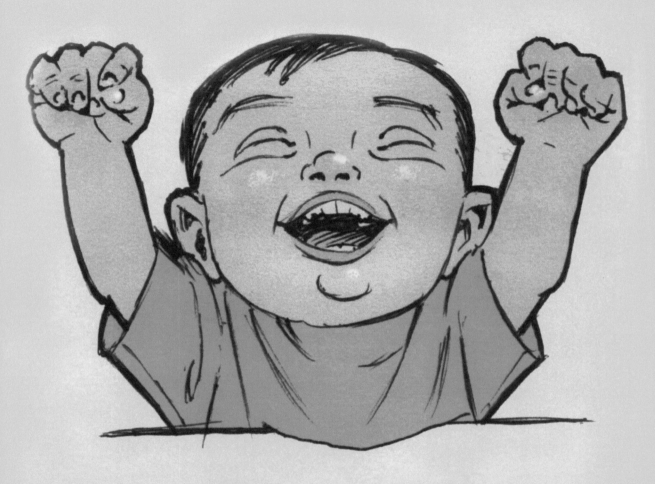

this is my winning face

this is my losing face

this
is
my
happy
face

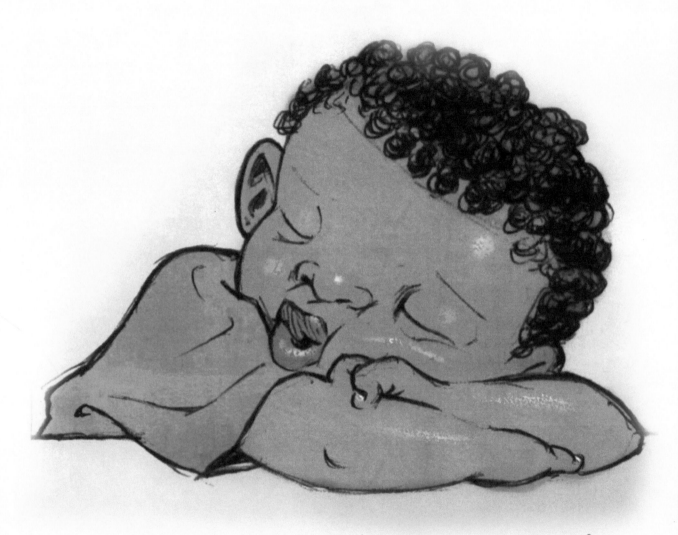

this is my nappy face

this is my
grampy
face

this is my monkey face

this is my Stinky face

this is my hungry face

this is my yawning face

my mommy and daddy love all my faces

CPSIA information can be obtained
at www.ICGtesting.com
Printed in the USA
LVHW071046011118
595592LV00013BA/92/P